A Black Pool Opened up at
My Feet and I Dived in

A BLACK POOL OPENED UP AT MY FEET AND I DIVED IN

Film Noir:
the cinematic language of 1940s America

Tim Young

Copyright © Tim Young 2024

All rights reserved. No part of this publication may be reproduced, stored in a retrieval system, or transmitted in any form or by any means, electronic, mechanical, photocopying, recording, or otherwise, without written permission of the publisher.

ISBN: 9798325759079

For permission to reproduce excerpts, use copyrighted material, translate, or adapt this work, please contact the auhor or publisher.

Ten Desert Island Films Noirs

The Maltese Falcon
Double Indemnity
Murder My Sweet
The Big Sleep
The Postman Always Rings Twice
The Killers
Crossfire
Out Of The Past
The Third Man
Sunset Boulevard

Another ten, worthy of further exploration

The Glass Key
Phantom Lady
The Woman In The Window
Laura
The Blue Dahlia
Gilda
Nightmare Alley
Dead Reckoning
Lady in the Lake
Act Of Violence

Ten B pictures of note

Stranger on the Third Floor
Street Of Chance
Strangers In The Night
Detour
Suspense
T Men
Raw Deal
Ride The Pink Horse
The Narrow Margin
Gun Crazy

Table of Contents

Influences	15
Source Material	26
Not Quite Noir	31
Settings and Structures	35
Ways of Showing	44
Antiheroes and Antiheroines	51
Contemporary Concerns	57
The 1950s	65
Classic?	71
Twelve Films Which Take Film Noir into and Through the 1950s	101
Bibliography	102
Acknowledgements	104

Over the past thirty years, the adjective "noir" has become a casual cultural shorthand. Films, television series and novels which portray darkness in some form are readily labelled: "neo-noir", "Scandi-noir" and even "Ozark Noir" and "Tartan-noir". A recent reviewer of JG Ballard's non-fiction credited him with inventing "bourgeois noir". *Breaking Bad* has been described as "the glorious darkness of Noir TV". One reviewer placed the French television series *Engrenages* ("Spiral") "within the jet-black context of Euro-noir". The term is felt to be sufficiently understood that it can be used in ways undreamed of by the French critics who coined it over seventy years ago; its deployment is not limited to the creative arts. A website for Stressless sofas and recliners bills its range of "Modern Noir": "Dark wood floors, inky walls and full-height curtains serve as a beautiful canvas when creating an intimate and poetic home with a dramatic and stylish atmosphere......Somehow your senses become more awake when you surround yourself with dark colours." Wilson invites the tennis player to "Make a statement with the limited-edition Film Noir Performance Tennis Racket Collection ".

There can be a time lag between an artistic period and general acceptance of its collective description. The Renaissance is a nineteenth century term for a fifteenth century phenomenon. The Arts Decoratifs Exhibtion in Paris was held in 1925, yet the term "art deco" did not appear in print until 1966. Although individual French writers were identifying particular American films as films noirs during what is seen as the "Classic" period between 1940 and 1959, this collective description did not take hold in the English-speaking world until the 1970s and the 1980s. The director Billy Wilder told his biographer in the 1990s: "I never heard that expression, film noir, when I made Double Indemnity. We didn't think we were working for forever, whatever "forever" is. I just made pictures I would have liked to see." Another director, Edward Dmytryk, remembered in a 1980s interview: " A student at the college said 'Tell me about film noir.' I said 'What's film noir?' We were just doing what came naturally."

American films were banned throughout France after 1942 and this deprivation during the Occupation meant that, once liberated, the French fell on new American culture in the shape of books, films and jazz. In September 1945, Gallimard, the French publishing house, produced a "Collection" of tough American novels and French-authored versions in the American style: this was known as the"Serie Noire". Films based on similar source material now reached France too, a year or more after their release in the USA: *The Maltese Falcon* (1941), Wilder's *Double Indemnity* and Dmytryk's *Murder My Sweet* (both 1944). In the summer of 1946, *Laura* (1944) and *The Woman In The Window (*1944) were also showing in France. This small cluster of American films represented "a major class of films which has superseded the Western", in the words of the critic Nino Frank.

France had a network of film clubs and film journals, which helped to generate an interest in seeing cinema as art rather than just as commercial entertainment. In attaching the adjective "noir" to these five recent arrivals in French cinemas, two 1946 magazine articles, one by Nino Frank, launched the European description of "a new kind of American film". There was a French tradition of stylistic identification: the early writers on film noir tapped into Existentialist and Surrealist ways of seeing. Frank's article appeared in "L'écran français" (a socialist-leaning magazine founded by the Resistance during the war, which continued after it). He emphasised the sense of difference: "these 'dark' films, these films noirs, no longer have anything in common with the ordinary run of detective movies". He distinguished them from dark French films of the 1930s in their "rejection of sentimental humanism" and he placed as a central feature "the dynamism of violent death". Jean-Pierre Chartier's essay, from November 1946, appeared in the conservative-leaning Revue du cinema, titled "Les Américains aussi font des films 'noirs'" ("the Americans also make 'black' films"). Chartier saw the "pessimism and disgust for humanity" as the common thread of film noir.

Two more French writers, Raymonde Borde and Etienne Chaumeton, expanded the idea of film noir in their 1955 book "Panorama du film noir americain". Borde and Chaumeton describe a number of "sources" of film noir: the hard-boiled crime novel; greater interest in "dynamic psychology" and in the work of psychiatrists; artistic exploitation of violence during and after World War Two, with a synthesis between realism and cruelty; European strands of Surrealism and Expressionism; and development from particular film genres in the 1930s (gangster, horror and detective). They highlighted the eroticised treatment of violence and the subversion of male and female leading roles. Borde and Chaumeton's interest in Surrealism encouraged them to emphasise the dreamlike quality of film noir. When, in the late 1950s, the French developed their own "new wave" of film-making (whose leading figures, Jean-Luc Godard, Eric Rohmer and Claude Chabrol, had started out as writers for the film magazine "Cahiers du Cinema"), interest in American films faded, but "Panorama du film noir americain", a key work, followed Frank and Chartier in laying foundations for later discussion of film noir.

It took almost twenty-five years from those first two articles in 1946 for what were known as "crime pictures" to be redefined in widespread popular perception as a coherent genre. English-language critics and film-makers in the late 1960s and early 1970s (notably Charles Higham, Raymond Durgnat and Paul Schrader) followed up those earlier French writers in drawing out noir's stylistic and thematic features as they saw them. The reappearance of American films noirs came in the 1970s in the form of "arthouse noir", films for the mainstream market, made by younger directors ("the film school generation") with a conscious reference to the style and age of the past: *Point Blank* (a 1967 forerunner from the British director, John Boorman), *Targets*, *Klute*, *The French Connection* (influenced by Howard Hawks), *Mean Streets* (whose title was taken from Raymond Chandler), *Chinatown* (Robert Towne attributed the script's origins to a magazine article on Chandler's Los Angeles), *Night Moves*, *Taxi Driver* (Paul Schrader again), *The Driver*, *Body Heat*, *Blood Simple* (from a Dashiell Hammett phrase), and, later, *The Grifters*, *The Usual Suspects*, *Miller's Crossing* (a reworking of Hammett's The Glass Key) and *Heat*. Popular film criticism from the later 1970s and 1980s onwards made the term "film noir" widespread in film vocabulary, style and art.

There were a great many films made from 1928 to 1948, the first two decades of sound cinema. Production was encouraged by the practice of block booking, a distribution tactic whereby the studios compelled exhibitors to take a package of B pictures alongside the A picture(s) they were keen to have. This practice was eventually outlawed by the Supreme Court, ruling against Paramount in 1948. (United States versus Paramount Pictures Inc was a landmark decision, creating the Paramount Decree, which separated film production companies from exhibition companies, with significant consequences.) The best-known films noirs were marketed as A pictures, with substantial budgets and well-known stars, but the sheer number of B films of all kinds ensured that films noirs can be found in forgotten corners. Critics argue about how many films noirs there were: the Film Noir Encyclopaedia of 1998 lists 317 titles, while Paul Duncan's Pocket Guide to Film Noir lists over 500 films, produced in the US between 1940 and 1960 and Michael F Keaney finds 745 films from the same "classic era 1940-1959". Those who made the films would have been surprised by the amount of critical scrutiny applied to their tightly-disciplined commercial offerings. This recognition through retrospective (with some nostalgia) is central to our modern understanding. By looking closely at those films from the 1940s and early 1950s, one can perhaps strip away these subsequent layers and observe what was distinctive about them in their own time and place.

This lack of agreement over the number of films noirs illustrates the problem of definition. Film noir was described as a "series" by Borde and Chaumeton, a "movement", "period", "tone" and "mood" by Paul Schrader, a "genre" by Charles Higham, a "motif" by Raymond Durgnat, a "scheme" by David Thomson, and elsewhere a "phenomenon", a "canon", a "transgeneric phenomenon", a "visual style", "the fugitive footage of postwar America", and even a set of "patterns of nonconformity". More broadly, films noirs were "movies about adults, made for adults who had just been through a war".

James Naremore, an American academic, described film noir as "an unusually baggy concept, elaborated largely after the fact of the films themselves....the beating heart of film noir can be located in Hollywood during the 1940s and 1950s. This was a period when the industry turned out modest, relatively unsung thrillers, often produced according to formula and released without fanfare, that were nearly

Tim Young | 13

always worth seeing." They were worth seeing, because they were, as Borde and Chaumeton saw, more than just good stories. They were products of cultural cross-fertilisation, expressed with skill, imagination and technical experience, reflecting the age in which the stories were set.

Ian Nathan, a British film critic, sees film noir as a form of expression. I would expand this to describe film noir as an enduring cinematic language: the use of film-making techniques, styles and ideas to bring new dimensions to a contemporary story which includes dark themes and complex characters, usually coloured by ambiguity, the rootlessness of urban life and the nihilism of World War Two. This establishes films noirs as distinctive, of their time, and worthy of examination in their own right. This was a unique coming together of particular source material, film-making expertise and the contemporary mood.

Influences

While a new generation of film school directors were behind the noir revival in the 1970s, the directors who made the original noir films in the 1940s were also comparatively young and products of film schooling of a different kind, namely, an immersion in European cinema and theatre. Boris Ingster (*Stranger on the Third Floor*) came originally from Riga and had worked with Sergei Eisenstein, the great Russian director. Edgar Ulmer (*Detour*, *The Strange Woman*) had done set design for Max Reinhardt, the pre-eminent Austrian theatre director, and worked with Expressionist film director FW Murnau. Fritz Lang was older, but brought with him his experience of German cinema in the Weimar years. Otto Preminger had also worked closely with Reinhardt, while Billy Wilder was a successful screenwriter in Berlin in his mid-twenties. Robert Siodmak directed the last silent German film and the first UFA sound film, working with Wilder and Ulmer. Gustav Machaty (*Jealousy*) had directed Hedy Lamarr in *Extase* in 1933 to international acclaim.

Those with European backgrounds were also important in shaping the visual and aural style of film noir. Rudolf Mate, impressive cinematographer for *Gilda*, came from a Polish-Hungarian background and had been the cameraman for the Danish directing giant Carl Dreyer,. John Alton was the first Hungarian-born cameraman to win an Academy

Award. Max Steiner, Miklos Rosza and Franz Waxman brought European musical sonorities to these films.

In addition to youth and European influence, the great age of American silent cinema was another strand in noir film-makers' backgrounds (a connection explored in *Sunset Boulevard*). Edward Dmytryk had been a messenger at Famous Players Lasky, while still at Hollywood High School (and had worked as projectionist, editor and director before he turned 31). Paul Ivano, whose photography lit up *The Shanghai Gesture*, *The Suspect* and *The Strange Affair of Uncle Harry*, had worked with distinctive silent directors (von Stroheim, von Sternberg and Rex Ingram), as had John Seitz, Wilder's cinematographer. Nicholas Musuraca, another fine director of photography, had begun as chauffeur to a producer of silents and then served a long apprenticeship in 1920s films.

There were notably influential art directors with longevity in the film business. Cedric Gibbons began with *Ben Hur* in 1925 and was nominated for an Academy Award (whose statuettes he had designed) thirty-nine times. Van Nest Polglase studied Beaux Arts architecture in New York and worked on the Presidential Palace in Havana before coming to Hollywood, having credits for over 300 films between 1925 and 1957. His contribution to *Citizen Kane* marks him out as an important figure in the development of the noir look. As a crowning illustration of the potential combination of European and American silent cinema, FW Murnau made *Sunrise* in 1927, named as the fifth best film of all time by the critics in Sight and Sound's 2012 poll, and described by David Thomson as a key step towards film noir.

The noir creators of the 1940s portrayed society's mood, as did their successors, who operated in the wake of social and political upheaval in the 1960s. Films noirs reflected, in different ways, the Great Depression, the gangster era and the world at war. Contemporary films about the Depression are thin on the ground: just three, *I Am A Fugitive From A Chain Gang*, *Of Mice And Men*, and *The Grapes Of Wrath*, stand out from the 1930s and the early 1940s. Audiences were more interested in being entertained, in escapism. In *Mildred Pierce*, the Depression and Prohibition had been features of the novel, but, interestingly, were absent from the film. If the Depression is more prominent in the source novels than the films, nonetheless it was clearly important in shaping the thinking of film noir protagonists. *Detour* (1945) illustrates very clearly the lingering influence of the Depression.

Gangster films enjoyed a short-term boom in the early 1930s (after the success of *Little Caesar* in 1931 showed studios that crime films paid): 9 were made in 1930, 26 in 1931, 28 in 1932 and 15 in 1933. Concern that these films might be harmful to those who saw them (a concern heightened by reports of cinema audiences cheering the gangster) led to a backlash, with Jack Warner announcing that his studio, Warner Brothers, would no longer make such films, along with local censorship, and stronger enforcement of the Motion Picture Production Code after 1934. James Cagney's move from violent gangster to law enforcer in films such as *G-Men* (1935) and *I Am The Law* (1938) exemplified this shift. The legacy of gangster films in film noir can be seen in a stronger portrayal of violence, not least against women (Cagney's gangster character crushes a grapefruit in a woman's face in *The Public Enemy* and knocks another woman out in *Picture Snatcher*).

However, there are features of gangster films which do not readily connect with film noir, such as the clear delineation between right and wrong (although the complexity of the "hero's" character and the ambivalence of the audience's reaction to him or her could be seen as precursors of noir characterisation) and the total focus on the central character of the gangster in the former. The arrested emotional development of the gangster, who is sometimes explicitly childlike, is a continuing thread in crime films, from *Scarface* to *White Heat* to Scorsese. In films, gangsters were usually individual outlaws in the 1930s, but members of larger (sometimes national) crime organisations in the 1950s; 1940s crime films track this development through the decade, with the racketeering organisations in *Force Of Evil* and the sophisticated counterfeiting gang in *T Men* illustrating the direction of travel. *High Sierra* (1941) emphasises the isolation of the doomed gangster as opposed to the milieu in which he moves, making it more of a gangster film than an early film noir.

The Second World War is a pervasive background to film noir, even if some Californian films in the 1940s disregard the conflict altogether. It had been " an extraordinary horrible war. Concentration camps, slaughter, atomic bombs, people killed for nothing. That can make anybody a little pessimistic" (Abraham Polonsky). Although the USA had been spared the violence present in Europe and Asia, the worldwide feelings of uncertainty, futility and nihilism can be seen throughout the film noir canon. There is cynicism in the reporters' room in *Stranger On The Third Floor*: "too many people in the world anyway". John Garfield is scarred by his imprisonment in the Spanish Civil War in *The Fallen Sparrow*. Nihilism balances out the patriotism in *This Gun for Hire* and the despair brought to America from Europe can be seen in the doomed author in *Jealousy*.

Films noirs often highlighted the issues facing those who had served in the conflict. The returned GI fallen on hard times in *The Chase* is an example of so many American servicemen who came back with deep experiences, a changed mindset and at a loose end. William Bendix's Buzz in *The Blue Dahlia* is an (irretrievably?) damaged returnee, whose act of murder was ruled out of the film by the Navy (much to writer Raymond Chandler's consternation). *Somewhere In The Night* features a veteran dealing with amnesia, while *Dead Reckoning* finds Bogart looking to clear the name of a dead comrade. *Act of Violence* suggests that those making respectable post-war lives might not be able to escape choices made during the war. There are thoughtful insights in *Crossfire* into the damaging effect of war on the men who served: as a stimulus to hatred and aggression, as a disruptor of marriages and as trauma.

Some commentators have seen the appearance of film noir as a by-product of rising crime in society, but the figures do not bear that out. Homicide rates rose during the Depression (9.7 murders per 100,000), but drifted steadily down through the 1930s (6.4 per 100,000 by 1940) and down to around 5 per 100,000 by 1950, rising steadily thereafter. (In his book, "Mad As Hell", the historian Dominic Sandbrook makes a thoughtful analysis of the very significant increase in US crime in the two decades after 1965.) In wartime, calling up so many young Americans may have removed many potential perpetrators from the country; significantly, the crime rate in the UK rose by around 50% during the war, with a combination of the blackout and the arrival of large numbers of GIs (as both instigators and victims of crime). One aspect of crime which did increase during the war seems to have been crimes committed by young people: there were 20% more juveniles fingerprinted in the US in 1944 than in 1942 (possibly an indication of looser restraints within families and communities). If the crime rate did not increase in the 1940s, what was happening in the world might have, nonetheless, engendered a more tolerant view of crime and violence in the home country, which was then reflected in the material on film. Prostitution (*Scarlet Street, Deadline At Dawn, Fallen Angel, Crossfire, Thieves Highway, Act of Violence*), pornography (*The Big Sleep*),violent racism (*Crossfire*), sadistic official beating (*Kiss The Blood Off My Hands*), and extreme violence (*Brute Force*) appear in several film noirs.

Many of the emigre directors and cameramen in film noir had been influenced by German Expressionism (although Fritz Lang was keen to deny its influence on him). Expressionism in its broadest sense is the application of a subjective anti-naturalism to material, exaggerating and distorting to bring a greater emotional impact. The post-war chaos in Weimar Germany provided the backdrop to this emerging artistic style. *The Cabinet of Dr Caligari* (1921), with its stylised geometrical backdrops (the sets had had to be adjusted to the small size of the studios), its chiaroscuro contrasts of light and shade, and its dreamlike plotting, is regarded as the foundation film in German Expressionism. German filmmakers in the 1920s followed this by using setting, light and shadow to express the dark psychology of their protagonists. Additionally, the majority of major German films over the next few years moved away from location shooting and were fully filmed in studios, which placed more emphasis on set design and the atmosphere that could be created. Expressionism can certainly be seen as the parent of the visual style of noir, with its unnatural lighting of everyday locations and of people, its emphasis on night exteriors and its unsettling angles. These stylistic features were used to heighten the uncertainty, suspicion and pessimism in the plots. Robert Siodmak's *Phantom Lady* is a fine example of Expressionist visuals in noir, showing a complete mastery of light and shadow, tilted cameras creating Dutch angles, the depth of shots and the lighting of individuals. Siodmak's cinematographer, Elwood Bredell, also brought an Expressionist tone to *The Killers*, underlining how American technicians could absorb German influences. Anthony Mann's *Desperate* differentiates the noir view as it shifts tone in the first ten minutes from a well-lit scene of a newly married couple preparing an anniversary dinner to the shadows and harsh spotlight on a brutal gang planning a heist.

Chartier's use of "aussi" in his article's title ("Les Américains aussi font des films 'noirs'") implies an existing strain of French film noir. A review of Pierre Chenal's *Le Dernier Tourant* in 1939 (the first film version of "The Postman Always Rings Twice") described it as "another film noir which belongs to the sinister series which starts with *Les Bas-Fonds* and *Crime et Chatiment* and continues with *Pepe Le Moko* and *Le Quai des Brumes*...". There was a French literary tradition of fascination with the underclass in society (the Bas-Fonds), a fascination which found new ways of showing this in the 1920s and 1930s, often by emigres from Central Europe. Brassai's collection of photographs "Paris de Nuit" made a significant impact and Siodmak (a recurrent figure in film noir) was making films in France between 1933 and 1939. The poetic realism movement in 1930s French cinema focused on characters on the margins of society. There is a forerunner of noir's visual style in the backdrop of wet cobbles, foggy nightscapes and squalid lodging-houses in *Le Quai des Brumes* (with Eugene Schufftan as its cinematographer). French film-makers, like their noir counterparts, were using the medium's possibilities to give additional qualities to realistic source material from Zola and others. However, the connections should not be over-emphasised. Yearning and sentiment run through these French films, counterbalanced by violence; the tone of film noir is different, with cynicism and suspicion overlaying the sentiment. If one looks at one plot occurrence, suicide stemming from despair and fatalism features in a number of these French films, whereas, in noir, it is used in calculating fashion to implicate rivals in *Rage in Heaven* and *Leave Her To Heaven*. When poetic realism and noir strands collide, the sentiment of poetic realism remains dominant, as in *Moontide*.

The documentary movement and Italian neorealist cinema, both important strands in film-making in this era, have limited influence over film noir, given their precedence of realism over style. Pre-war documentaries aimed to infuse poetry and nobility into the (supposedly unacted) material they recorded, whether exotic life (the work of Robert Flaherty, *Song of Ceylon*) or daily work (Grierson's *Drifters*, *Night Mail*). Wartime documentary films, exemplified by Frank Capra's *Why We Fight* series (seen by almost 60 million Americans), did have some influence in the later 1940s and 1950s: the authoritative voice-over with an implicit presentation of truths, the portrayal of teamwork by government servants with a moral common purpose, and the idea of large crowds of people out there. Italian cinema could reflect American culture: *Ossessione* (1942) was Visconti's use of noir source material (James M Cain's "The Postman Always Rings Twice" once again), while the posters being put up in *Bicycle Thieves* were for *Gilda*. However, the neorealists' use of non-professional actors and their frequent focus on childhood were not salient features of film noir. The difficulties of distribution impeded significant exposure to neorealism in the US, but, here again, one can see some influence in the location shooting which became common in what can be termed docunoir. *The Naked City*, a memorable love letter to New York, shows the influence of Italian neorealism (as well as the photographs of Weegee, the iconic city photographer hired as a visual consultant).

In the first half of the twentieth century, psychiatry came into the mainstream of American awareness. Earlier, the instinct had been to label people as madmen and madwomen, confining them to institutions. Interestingly, in 1921, the American Journal of Insanity, which had commenced publication in 1844, changed its name to the American Journal of Psychiatry. In 1923, Thomas Salmon, prominent in military psychiatry during World War One, was elected President of the American Psychiatric Association: his predecessors had all been superintendents of mental asylums. Sigmund Freud published influential work in 1917 ("An Introduction to Psychoanalysis") and 1921 ("Group Psychology and Analysis of the Ego"). The American Medico-Psychological Association produced the first uniform classification of mental diseases in 1918. The newly-discovered phenomenon of shell shock in World War One had been important in this: when it came to the next war, of just under 2 million men rejected for military service, almost 40% were excluded on neuro-psychiatric grounds. All of this was to play a part in the subject matter and tone of film noir. Lines like "I found your monograph on mental telepathy and intuition most interesting" (*The Night Has A Thousand Eyes*) could appear natural enough within noir dialogue.

The Motion Picture Production Code was drawn up by a Jesuit priest and a Catholic layman in 1929 and then adopted by the Motion Pictures Producers and Distributors Association (MPPDA) in 1930: the producers were amenable to central decision-making as a way of navigating the widely varying rulings of local censorship boards. An amendment in 1934 required all films released after July 1st of that year to obtain a certificate of approval before being released. The studios complied voluntarily over the following thirty years in order to avoid government censorship. The two figures most closely associated with the Code were Will Hays, Chairman of the MPPDA between 1922 and 1945, and Joseph Breen, a Catholic journalist in charge of the Production Code Administration (which issued the certificates) from its inception in 1934 to 1954 (with a brief spell away between 1941 and 1942). Under the Code, all criminal action had to be punished, sexual relations outside marriage would not be shown as permissible, sexual perversion (which included homosexuality) could not be portrayed, and authority figures (especially the clergy) must be respected.

Therefore, the age of film noir coincided with the strongest enforcement of such a code. This could have a negative effect on films, notably the artificiality of some endings (since malefactors could not be shown to have escaped just retribution) and the contrived deaths of villains (since murderers other than law enforcers could not escape justice). On the other hand, the Code forced film-makers to be creative. Joseph Breen was hostile to explicit portrayal: "When people talk about realism, they usually talk about filth". Borde and Chaumeton described the "paradoxically positive effect on film noir" in the need for confusion, eroticism and innuendo, with a dreamlike atmosphere, suggestive lighting and fetishised clothing. "The implied meaning can only add ....to the images' power of suggestion ." Director Edward Dmytryk later said that the Code "had a very good effect because it made us think. If we wanted to get something across that was censorable... we had to do it deviously. We had to be clever. And it usually turned out to be much better than if we had done it straight."

The studio system also provided a framework within which producers and directors had to work. Looking back in the 1970s, Howard Hawks reflected that "the studio system worked, because we couldn't be excessive, we couldn't do just what we wanted to do". The disjointed features of Orson Welles' *The Lady From Shanghai* (alongside moments of noir excellence) suggest that studio constraints often helped to bring a coherent and satisfying final outcome.

Welles' earlier masterpiece, *Citizen Kane*, was more of an influence for the young film-makers of the late 1960s and 1970s, but its footprint can be seen in film noir, even if it is very hard to find an explicit reference to it among noir directors, writers and cameramen. There may have been neither crime nor urban anonymity in the film, but the heavy Expressionist use of light and shade, the structure which builds a picture of a dead person through the perspectives of different characters, a complex and disillusioned central personality, the use of angles (those ceilings), the extra dimension provided by Bernard Herrmann's score, these all prefigured film noir in striking fashion. The look and decoration of *Citizen Kane* also anticipate noir: the use of mirrors, window patterns and Venetian blinds, the stylised sets (early and late views of Kane's Xanadu could have fitted seamlessly alongside the landscape of Dr Caligari), the combination of deep focus with intense chiaroscuro (the projection room and the Thatcher library), and the rainy streets where Kane meets Susan Alexander (the latter a noir femme fatale who finally takes decisive action). *Citizen Kane*, with its confident use of cinematic language, its structure and its style, was a natural prelude to film noir.

Source Material

"Chandler and Hammett were writing film noir before we made it." (Edward Dmytryk).

The source material of noir has been a major reason for the enduring appeal of the best of these films. "Hard-boiled" is the adjective generally used for the original novels and the principal authors were Raymond Chandler, Dashiell Hammett, James M Cain and Cornell Woolrich (with Graham Greene an honourable non-American addition). Woolrich (writing under several pseudonyms) has 103 screen credits, Chandler 37 and Hammett 33. James M Cain has fewer credits, but these include key noir texts in "Double Indemnity", "Mildred Pierce" and "The Postman Always Rings Twice". These men had hard-boiled life experiences: Woolrich lived alone in a seedy New York hotel after his mother died, Cain drifted through mundane jobs after college, while Hammett worked as a Pinkerton detective before turning to writing.

Sharp dialogue was an important and salient feature of the films. In making *The Maltese Falcon*, first-time director John Huston saw Hammett's prose as virtual scripts, with minimal description alongside the acerbic exchanges between characters. Bogart's Sam Spade's lines are certainly robust ("Mrs Spade didn't raise any children dippy enough to make guesses in front of a DA, an assistant DA and a stenographer", "I'm tired of being called things by every crackpot on the city payroll", "The cheaper the crook, the gaudier the patter","Why couldn't he have stayed alive long enough to tell us something?") while Sydney Greenstreet's fruity expostulations serve as counterpoint ("Well, sir, I must say you have a most violent temper", "You certainly are a most headstrong individual", "By Gad Sir you are a character").

The first half-hour of *The Big Sleep* has some of the sharpest dialogue in cinema history as Bogart's Marlowe bounces successively off Norris, the butler, Carmen Sternwood, General Sternwood, Vivian Sternwood Rutledge, and Agnes, the assistant at Geiger's Rare Books. This is followed by a delicately sexually charged scene at the Acme Bookstore, in its own way as provocative as the famous probing talk later between Bogart and Bacall. David Thomson describes General Sternwood as "high on words, like all of *The Big Sleep*, a picture in love with unanswerable talk....divine chatter". Chandler's atmospheric take on his adopted city of Los Angeles ("the quality of shady poetry" according to Dilys Powell) could not easily be portrayed on film, but his superb exchanges endure. Earlier, since James M Cain was contracted to another studio at the time *Double Indemnity* was being scripted, Chandler was brought in to help and his influence is evident in some of the teasing innuendo. "There's a speed limit in this state, Mr Neff..."

Jonathan Latimer's witty noir screenplays make him an honourable addition to this writers' group with over a dozen screenwriting credits in this era. Latimer was a former Chicago journalist and a crime novelist. His work included a screenplay for *The Glass Key* from Hammett's influential novel: "My first wife was a second rate cook in a third rate joint on Fourth street". In *The Big Clock*, a character spurns being in Who's Who "because he doesn't want his left hand to know whose pocket his right hand is picking". Latimer also reveals a modern sense of irony: "Whoever heard of a detective with his hat off?" (*Nocturne*).

The source material also establishes a distinctive landscape. Noir works well in an urban setting. Raymond Chandler's "The High Window" describes the "old town, lost town, shabby town, crook town….jigsaw Gothic mansions…all rooming houses now, their parquetry floors are all scratched and worn through, the once glossy finish and the wide sweeping staircases dark with time and with cheap varnish, laid on over generations of dirt. In the tall rooms haggard landladies bicker with shifty tenants. In and around the old houses there are flyblown restaurants and Italian fruit stands and cheap apartment houses and little candy stores where you can buy even nastier things than their candy. And there are ratty hotels where nobody except people named Smith and Jones sign the register." Noir in a European context could include the damage done by war: Graham Greene sets up his "background…the smashed dreary city of Vienna...a city of undignified ruins which turned that February into great glaciers of snow and ice".

"Hard-boiled" writing brought in characters ready to be portrayed vividly and memorably on film. Once again, Raymond Chandler's observational writing translated perfectly to the screen. We meet Sheriff Patton from "The Lady in the Lake": "A man sat at the desk in a wooden armchair whose legs were anchored to flat boards, fore and aft, like skis…He had a sweat-stained Stetson on the back of his head and his large hairless hands were clasped comfortably over his stomach, above the waistband of a pair of khaki pants that had been scrubbed thin years ago. His shirt matched the pants except that it was even more faded. It was buttoned tight to the man's thick neck and undecorated by a tie. His hair was mousy-brown, except at the temples where it was the colour of old snow…He had large ears and friendly eyes and his jaws munched slowly…I liked everything about him".

Cornell Woolrich has over one hundred screen credits: his stories transferred readily to film. Woolrich brought coincidence into his novels, layering sudden misfortune, amnesia and nightmares into criminal encounters. His biographer described "the most wretched life of any American writer since Poe". James M Cain's work could take some time to get to screen, since it was often seen as unfilmable within the Production Code: Joseph Breen vowed that he would never allow "The Postman Always Rings Twice" to be turned into a film. However, the novels were swiftly bought by studios and the films were made by turning the adulterous sex into memorable verbal interplay. Cain's central theme of yielding to forbidden desire fitted in with several plot strands of noir: the femme fatale, men taken helplessly out of their depth, erotic suggestion, and dark criminality which leads to retribution. Although a good plot made a story attractive to potential film-makers, it can be the dialogue, the atmosphere and the characters in much of the source material which give the films their particular qualities, a reason why the best of these films can be enjoyed more than once.

Graham Greene's film credits are also numerous, with over 30 cinema and television adaptations of 22 novels, more than any other major novelist. He had four and a half formative years reviewing films for the Spectator and for Night and Day magazine (closed after litigation following his unwise remarks about Shirley Temple). Basil Wright, the director, described Greene's "built-in filmic style". Greene had it all: telling dialogue, the noir backdrop of Greeneland (seen by Greene's biographer as "a province of The Waste Land"), and a keen interest in people (Greene averred that "a story without characters cannot succeed"). James Naremore emphasises Greene's veneration of French films about the bas-fonds, his concept of "blood-melodrama" as a rebellion against "middle-class virtues", and the recurrence of angelic killers identified by Borde and Chaumeton. Greene's plots were immediately attractive to film-makers. Paramount bought "A Gun for Sale" on publication in the US, Fritz Lang was keen to make "Ministry of Fear" by "one of his favourite writers ", and Alexander Korda wanted Greene to write a film treatment about the aftermath of war in a European city. (This treatment, which became a novella, emerged from a paragraph written by Greene on an envelope flap twenty years before.) Film noir coincided with the high point of Greene's written output: both were to benefit.

Not Quite Noir

In their groundbreaking book, Borde and Chaumeton differentiate between the crime film noir (looking at crime from the criminal's perspective) and the police procedural noir (looking from the law enforcer's perspective). The latter is concerned with establishing and reporting truths (as *Call Northside 777's* opening credits underline), while the former hovers on the edge of a dream (both the criminal's doomed dream and the pervasive sense of hallucination or nightmare). The police procedural is often signalled by an authoritative voice-over (owing much to the March of Time newsreels) and shot in semi-documentary style. The heroes are morally upright and impossible to corrupt: their leadership of their team is admirable, as opposed to the double-cross tendency in criminal gangs. (Glenn Ford, square of jaw, is much more interesting as the amoral adventurer in *Gilda* than as the happily-married honest government agent in *The Undercover Man*.) These films are designed to reassure (and have dated more noticeably than dark noirs). They are not without interest, but they are not examined in detail in this study. Borde and Chaumeton distinguished them from noirs by calling them police documentaries.

There are, nonetheless, police documentaries whose artistic qualities shine. The Time Out reviewer wrote of *T Men* (1947) that "it effortlessly transcends its semi-documentary brief to land deep in noir territory. John Alton's superlative camerawork counterpoints tensions and perspectives with almost geometrical precision." The dark criminal underworld in which the undercover agents move is brilliantly portrayed by a combination of Anthony Mann's direction and Alton's photography, but the narrator anchors the whole within a framework approved by government. J Edgar Hoover's involvement in *The House on 92nd Street* is another illustration of using noir techniques in the service of an official narrative.

Early in the 1940s, there were a number of plays which were used as noir source material, but they tend to produce stage-bound rather than cinematic productions. To these eyes, *Casablanca*, for all its many merits and the accomplished direction of Michael Curtiz, still shows its stage origins (whereas *The Maltese Falcon* and *The Big Sleep* have a cinematic fluidity, despite their evident studio sets). In part, it is the grand central space depicted on film which harks back to the play's original setting: Rick's Cafe in *Casablanca*, the house on the marshes in *Ladies In Retirement*, the shadowy dockside in *Out Of The Fog*, the main family room in *The Strange Affair of Uncle Harry*, and the huge gaming house in *The Shanghai Gesture*. It is not essential to have the action played out in dark rainy streets, but these proscenium locations tend to conjure up a theatrical atmosphere.

Similarly, Southern locations brought a different, somewhat Gothic, shading to their films. *Dark Waters* and *Christmas Holiday*, both released in 1944, have a number of characteristically noir features (nightmare immersion and noir regulars in Thomas Mitchell and Elisha Cook in the former, sharp dialogue and Siodmak's use of shadows in the latter), but the overall tone is of Southern melodrama. Period films also inhabit a separate space from authentic noir. *Hangover Square* and *The Lodger*, both with John Brahm directing and

Laird Cregar in memorable central performances, have Expressionist power, but portray aberration within a comfortable settled society in another age, rather than giving us a feel for contemporary urban rootless angst (where crime is something of an expected occurrence). *The Suspect* is beautifully directed by Siodmak and photographed by Ivano, but it is an ordered world (middle-class Edwardian London) with conventions and expectations, not an uncertain and shifting landscape of cynicism and betrayal.

Alfred Hitchcock made a number of memorable films during the principal noir period. These have many noir features. However, Hitchcock's preoccupations, the films' settings and the straightforward style of storytelling place his films outside this study of film noir. Hitchcock liked to portray the introduction of menace to a small town (his personal favourite, *Shadow of a Doubt*) or to a blonde woman or to both. *Suspicion* is set in country house society and Waxman's music reinforces the idea of a pastoral idyll (as opposed to his work in other films noirs). *Rebecca* has some film noir identifiers (a voice over, the music score, obsession, the atmospheric interiors), but it is more in the tradition of Hollywood's interest in the British upper classes (as with "Jane Eyre" and "Wuthering Heights"). *Strangers On A Train*, with its stylised opening and disorienting murder sequence in an amusement park, is probably the Hitchcock film which can be placed most comfortably in the noir canon.

In 1947, only 12% of the films made in the US were made in colour. The expense of colour meant that it was only used for particular (non-animated) genre show-pieces: musicals, historical romances and swashbucklers. Technicolor (with its bulky cameras and added expense) had a tendency to soften focus as the light passed through the three strips in the process. Technicolor was thus not equipped for noir, as indicated in James Agee's review of *Leave Her To Heaven*: "The story's central idea might be plausible enough in a dramatically lighted black and white picture, or in a radio show. But in the rich glare of Technicolor, all its rental-library characteristics are doubly jarring." (TIME magazine, 7 January 1946). The expense and technical limitations of colour help to explain the predominance of black and white in 1940s crime films. By 1954, after the introduction of the "single-strip process" (which could fit into any 35mm camera), over half of the films made in Hollywood were in Eastmancolor. Deep focus in colour was now possible, even if shadow remained elusive: noir needs the expressive potential of chiaroscuro. The magnificent restoration of *Gilda* reveals the full glory of black and white film noir. The arrival of Eastmancolor in the 1950s may have been an additional factor in providing an endpoint to the great age of film noir. There were still striking black and white noir films in the mid and late 1950s, but Expressionism in colour could now be found, as demonstrated by Elia Kazan's *East of Eden* and the films of Douglas Sirk.

Settings and Structures

Contemporary urban settings suit film noir: it could be said that they help to define film noir. Anthony Mann's *Two O'Clock Courage* has the quintessential noir opening as a bleeding man (with amnesia) leans on a street sign in an unnamed city in hazy light at night. Cities provided anonymity, alienation, rootlessness and darkness, whereas rural communities stood for stability, a settled environment in which everyone knows everyone else. Noir cities are anywhere, not somewhere. Often unidentified, they do not speak to a particular place, even when named: *The Maltese Falcon's* opening shot of the Golden Gate Bridge, with the title San Francisco, has no real connection to the rest of the film. The photographs of Alfred Stieglitz and the paintings of Edward Hopper provide parallel contemporary expressions of shadowy solitude in the American city: Abraham Polonsky gave his cameraman, George Barnes, a book of Hopper's Third Avenue paintings to indicate the look he wanted for *Force Of Evil*. The city bar into which a fugitive Van Heflin stumbles in *Act of Violence* is straight out of the famous scene in Hopper's Nighthawks painting.

This noir convention of a surreal hunt through an unfriendly urban landscape, sometimes by unknown pursuers, was established in *This Gun For Sale* and repeated frequently, as in *Street Of Chance, Odd Man Out, The Third Man*, and *Night and the City*. Nicholas Christopher sees the city as a labyrinth, with the protagonist's voice-over charting an uncertain route through that labyrinth (sometimes from a dead, dying or near-death perspective, as in *Sunset Boulevard*, *DOA* and *Murder My Sweet*). There are noirs which do have a sense of place (San Francisco or New York in several films, Billy Wilder's Los Angeles, Carol Reed's Vienna or Belfast), but the tendency to shoot in studios generally sets noir's mean streets in universal cities.

Film noir characters often live in dark rooms in tenement buildings, accentuating the anonymity of their city existence. The plot of *Stranger On The Third Floor* centres around these living arrangements, while shabby boarding-houses feature in the Graham Greene adaptations (*This Gun For Hire*, *Brighton Rock*). The revival of city entertainment after the combination of Prohibition and the Depression provided communal settings which were natural backdrops for vice, corruption and crime: by 1946, there were 70,000 night clubs in the US. The flourishing of criminality behind a legitimate front is illustrated in *I Walk Alone* by the transformation of The Four Regents speakeasy into The Regent Club and Kirk Douglas's move from bootlegger to soft-living night club owner with legal weapons to hand ("No hiding behind peepholes, this is big business"). Gambling remained largely illegal in the US (although Nevada had permitted gambling in 1931 to generate income during the Depression), so casinos were either overseas locations (*The Shanghai Gesture*) or illegal dens (*Hollow Triumph*).

These films are set in somewhere without community, but they can be in a place where the community and fabric have been disrupted and destroyed, usually by war. When film noir meets rubble film, it adds an extra layer of dislocation and nihilism, as in *Three Strangers*, in *Kiss The Blood Off My Hands*, in *Odd Man Out* (where bomb sites and an air raid shelter are key locations early in the film), in *Berlin Express*, and in *The Third Man*. Inevitably, this occurs in European locations rather than American noir. Night is also a central element in these settings: the key scenes in *The Third Man* take place at night, while *Odd Man Out* portrays the events of a single night. The opening title of *Kiss The Blood Off My Hands* reads "The aftermath of war is rubble - the rubble of cities and of men".

Action in Latin America brings an additional sense of otherness and dislocation to several films noirs. *Gilda* in Buenos Aires, Kathie in Acapulco in *Out Of The Past*, the secret organisation in *Cornered*, the Havana dystopia in *The Chase*, and the monstrous characters in the border town in *Touch Of Evil* all operate largely outside the rules, in locations where American assumptions and codes have been left behind. Spanish-speaking America is different: sometimes threatening, sometimes a place where fascist authorities exert a corrupt influence, sometimes a moonlit paradise (and an ultimate sanctuary, as in *Dark Passage*). When Dick Powell's wife in *Pitfall* reminds him of the alternative to his humdrum life in insurance, she says "They've got a road that goes all the way to South America". In *Raw Deal*, the fugitive convict speaks of buying land and raising children in South America just as we learn, through the narration of his girlfriend, that her revelation will prevent their ever getting there. Lisabeth Scott in *Too Late for Tears* makes it to Mexico where she starts spending her loot, but she backs over a balcony (when cornered) and lies dead with the dollar notes floating around her.

Occasionally, mean city streets are deliberately contrasted with a rural idyll, possibly unattainable, possibly somewhere where one's urban misdeeds inevitably catch up with one (*Out Of The Past*, *The Killers*, *The Asphalt Jungle*). The depiction of city criminals invading a peaceful rural community is striking in *Desperate* (and remains a trope in subsequent cinema, as in Peter Weir's *Witness*).

"Yes, this is Sunset Boulevard, Los Angeles, California. It's about five o'clock in the morning." Alternatively: "I shall never forget the weekend Laura died. A silver sun burned through the sky like a huge magnifying glass. It was the hottest Sunday in my recollection. I felt as if I were the only human being left in New York. For with Laura's horrible death, I was alone." Or even: "I never knew the old Vienna before the war with its Strauss music, its glamour and its easy charm. Constantinople suited me better. I really got to know it in the classic period of the black market." Despite the tradition of theatrical narration, the central importance of image in the silent cinema and afterwards meant that narrators in film have been regarded with suspicion, as a device to compensate for a failure in showing. However, noir voice-overs enhanced their films, adding a combination of background introduction and a personal perspective: the latter draws the viewer in, providing additional engagement to the images which tell the story. We feel a personal connection with the narrator, even when, as with Walter Neff in *Double Indemnity*, he is not behaving at all well. The first two-thirds of *Dead Reckoning* are narration to a priest, inhabiting Bogart's thought processes in his quest. Sometimes, as in *Murder My Sweet*, the words echo the sharp dialogue within the film: "A black pool opened up at my feet and I dived in". They can infuse dramatic irony, as when we know the final fate of Joe Gillis in *Sunset Boulevard* from the start of the film. They can lead the viewer down a false trail. The personal viewpoint given by the narrator can call its reliability into question: the solo male voice-over in *Detour* (where the novel has both a male and a female narrator) raises the question as to whether the driver's death might, after all, have been murder. Noir cinema elevates the possibility of the voice-over: the heightened personal sense from narration recurs with distinction in later cinema, such as in the earlier films of Woody Allen and Terrance Malick.

The use of flashback in film structures has become a commonplace, whether in 1960s epics (*Lawrence of Arabia*, *Doctor Zhivago*), in the films of Quentin Tarantino, or in long-form television (*Better Call Saul*, *The White Lotus*). It acts as a hook, encouraging a discovery of how the characters and the narrative reached that endpoint. Films in the 1930s had used flashback as a similar and simple opening framing device for narrative (*Beau Geste*, *Lost Horizon*), but flashback became much more personal and fragmented after *Citizen Kane* and in film noir. Flashbacks become windows into the minds of the protagonist or participants, rather than pure narrative frames for a linear story. *Citizen Kane* introduced the idea of flashbacks reflecting different perspectives on the same person or incident. In *Detour*, focus on a surreally enlarged coffee cup and a juke box heralds a tortured flashback. The internal voice-over in *The Big Clock* introduces the flashback to 36 hours earlier and alters the whole tone of the rest of the film. Repeated voice-overs during the flashback, as in *Double Indemnity* and *Murder My Sweet*, sustain a personal perspective on events: Adrian Scott, the producer of *Murder My Sweet*, wanted to include the voiced flashback to retain the first-person style of Chandler's novel. *The Locket* in 1947 proved an extreme example, with a flashback within a flashback within a flashback, each one sufficiently subjective to raise some doubt about the honesty of the raconteur.

Searching for an elusive (and often dead) central character through flashbacks from different perspectives is a further development of this noir structure, pioneered in bravura form by Welles' *Citizen Kane*. *Laura* and *The Killers* show how this can deepen the film's narrative, engaging the viewer in the quest. Subjective flashbacks to the same sequence of events begin to realign the narrative in *Crossfire*. This imaginative approach to structure and character development was a lasting legacy to cinema. John Hodiak, as George Taylor in *Somewhere In The Night*, suffering from amnesia, tries to build a picture of himself through others' recollections of him.

In making the neo-noir *Body Heat*, Lawrence Kasdan said that he "wanted this film to have the intricate structure of a dream, the density of a good novel, and the texture of recognizable people in extraordinary circumstances"; this could serve as a template for classic film noir. The Maltese Falcon is described as "the stuff that dreams are made of". Lisabeth Scott to Bogart in *Dead Reckoning:* "Where have we met?" "In another guy's dreams." The world of dreams is central to *The Cabinet of Dr Caligari* and it is also a central feature in many films noirs, notably when they are based on the writings of Cornell Woolrich, where the narrative often veers into nightmare. Dreams are another means of allowing the viewer inside the mind of the main protagonist, reflecting noir's play on popular ideas about psychiatry. Dreams connect with a Surreal view of the world, something in which Borde and Chaumeton were particularly interested. They used "oneiric" (dreamlike) as a frequent descriptor of noir narratives. Despite the clumsy ending of *The Woman in the Window*, Lang's directorial skill has already put us into the mind of Edward G Robinson's Professor throughout the film, replacing sharp dialogue with a cinematic imagining of his thoughts. Dreams and reality are so closely and stylistically integrated in many films noirs (as in *Fear In The Night*) that the whole film can seem dreamlike (and sometimes proves to be so). Orson Welles declared that "the cinema has no boundary. It is a ribbon of dream".

The ultimate twist in a film noir sees a character returning from supposed death. This happens in artful ways in several films, dramatically altering our understanding from the first part of the film. It might be a case of mistaken identity (accidental or deliberate) or it might be a deliberately faked death. In *Strange Illusion*, the protagonist imagines (or is) receiving letters from his dead father (although the latter stays dead). Grief after World War One and the post-war flu pandemic had helped to stir belief in communication with the dead, usually through spiritualism, although there was no corresponding surge during and after the Second World War. In addition, the relatives of those "Missing In Action" would have hoped to be surprised by the return of their loved ones. It may be that the reversal of death in noir was merely a plot device, but it probably also chimed with a heartfelt wish in many contemporary audiences.

Films noirs do not, as a rule, outstay their welcome. B pictures are not much longer than an hour (*Strangers In The Night* is only 55 minutes). This encourages an economy of film language. Editing can make for quick exposition, as with the swift procession of images in *Jealousy*, from police department to court to jail. Films noirs set out their stall briskly (*The Big Sleep*) and denouements often have an even faster momentum (*My Name Is Julia Ross*). This pace of storytelling is another (welcome?) aspect of the cinematic language of film noir. The overblown nature of some mid-1950s cinema (*The Ten Commandments*, *Around The World In 80 Days*) brought a critical reaction in favour of economy of expression and production. This led to a measure of veneration for many B pictures: respect for *Detour* rested in part on the (false) belief that it had been shot in 6 days at a cost of £20,000.

Sometimes noir endings are hasty efforts to comply with the Code. Not allowing wrongdoers to get away with it (and removing the right to kill without retribution from those who are not law enforcers) led to a creative succession of deaths by misadventure: run over by a stray truck in *Stranger On The Third Floor*, falling off a boat in *Out of the Fog*, driven over a cliff by a suicidal driver in *Blues in the Night*, drowned off slippery rocks in *Moontide*, toppled by runaway horses in *The Strange Woman*, falling down a lift shaft in *The Big Clock* and so on. Alternatively, wrongdoers could commit suicide (*Phantom Lady*, *I Wake Up Screaming*, *Leave Her To Heaven*) or suffer eternal misery on earth (*Scarlet Street*). Sometimes the difficulty of allowing an essentially good person to escape justice was addressed by a hasty revelation that it had all been a dream (*The Woman in the Window*, *Fear*, *Black Angel*, *Strange Impersonation*, *The Strange Affair of Uncle Harry*): producer Joan Harrison was so angered by what she felt was Universal's feeble resort to this in the last of these that she decamped to RKO. B pictures could overdo the economy of storytelling by rushing the ending. *Detour*, *My Name Is Julia Ross* and *Strange Illusion* are all, I think, diminished by excessively swift denouements. Some of the more interesting endings in film noir are those where alternatives have been seriously considered: *Double Indemnity* (where the filmed gas chamber scene would have provided retribution for a murderer, but Wilder preferred to concentrate on the relationship between Neff and Keyes), *The Blue Dahlia* (requiring a change of murderer to placate the US Navy), *Mildred Pierce* (where a murder was inserted to stop the femme fatale from leaving with Mildred's husband for a new life) and *The Third Man* (Greene and Reed's disagreement over a happy or an unhappy ending). The layers of ambiguity in the final ten minutes of *Out Of The Past* provide a satisfying ending which stays with the cinemagoer. "Death's at the bottom of everything, Martins. Leave death to the professionals." (Major Calloway in *The Third Man*) Films noirs do not always place their trust in long-term incarceration; there is often a high body count. The finality of death provided neat endings, particularly when there would be no chance of a monster returning much later. The readiness to shoot to kill without hesitation might be a legacy of the gangster films and Westerns of a decade earlier or it might be another echo of the greater tolerance of extreme violence after World War Two. Transgressors in film noir were very lucky to escape with their lives. The early French critics focused on this feature of noir. Nino Frank's "dynamism of violent death" was echoed by Borde and Chaumeton: "Sordid or strange, death always emerges at the end of a tortuous journey. Film noir is a film of death, in all senses of the word".

Ways of Showing

Film noir used light and shadow to emphasise character and atmosphere: the resulting look is a noir signature. Big budget Hollywood films of the 1930s and 1940s had looked to give audiences a classically harmonious and objective view of the action, with centred compositions, smooth story editing, and the removal of shadows behind the principals by fill lighting at the sides. There were several reasons why film noir moved away from this style of presentation. The influence of Expressionist cinematography and staging was one, as emigre cinematographers and directors made their mark in the US. Improved technology, often accelerated by World War 2, was another reason: deep focus and wide angle lenses, more mobile cameras, and the possibility of night-for-night shooting (as opposed to creating a night effect with artificial lighting). Cost was a factor too: the three point lighting system was expensive and patches of darkness could mask cheaper sets. Without colour, it was important to light the foreground and background differently and to accentuate black and white in order to distinguish between the different objects on the screen. This chiaroscuro tendency in noir gave characters more mystery (as their faces were only partially lit) and the landscape in which they moved could seem unsettled and threatening. Noir also used unbalanced compositions, low angle and high angle shots, and extreme close ups to emphasise the subjectivity. These films aimed to engage on a personal level.

Dark Passage and *The Lady in the Lake*, both released in 1947, experimented with an even more subjective use of the camera, adopting the point of view of the hero (who is only seen in mirrors). This aimed to replicate the first person narrative of novels: "You'll see it just as I saw it" claims Phillip Marlowe (Robert Montgomery) at the start of *The Lady in the Lake*. It is an interesting (and memorable) ploy, but it lacks subtlety and it was not repeated. *Dark Passage* is the more successful film, because it varies the approach (depicting the hallucinating effect of anaesthetic, for example) and the camera switches to an objective point of view after an hour. Another effective instance in 1947, in *Possessed*, uses a subjective point of view as Joan Crawford is wheeled into hospital: this emphasises her unbalanced state of mind. Hallucination, nightmare and psychosis were the most frequent triggers of the shift to a personal camera point of view.

A variation on this subjectivity is the fluid moving camera, often at the beginning of the film, to bring the viewer into the scene. Russell Metty proved a master of this, with his opening shots in *Ride The Pink Horse* and (famously) in *Touch of Evil*. Improved technology and the ingenuity of directors of photography facilitated this immersion with James Wong Howe filming the boxing scenes in *Body and Soul* on roller skates inside the ring. In *Gun Crazy*, the view is from the back seat of a car, throughout the approach to a bank, during the tense moments as the armed robber is inside, and as the car gets away.

When Venetian blinds appear in a film, it is a sign that we are probably moving (or have already moved) into noir territory. Gobos are patterned screens placed in front of the camera to create these shadow effects, while cookies, further away from the light source, do the same. Blinds provide an additional and horizontal shading to the overall chiaroscuro, whether in a police station *(I Wake Up Screaming)*, in the house of seduction (*Double Indemnity*), in a cafe (*Fallen Angel*), viewed from a train window (*Lady on A Train*), in a psychiatrist's office (*Conflict*), a screen through which a camera moves (*Black Angel*), hiding a failed bathroom murder attempt (*The Postman Always Rings Twice*) or in a local newspaper office (*The Strange Love of Martha Ivers*). Once Barbara Stanwyck makes an appearance, it seems only a matter of time before she has Venetian blinds as a backdrop, a clear indication of her dark state of mind. Vertical stripes are also part of the iconography of noir, suggesting entrapment (and incarceration): they can be portrayed by prison bars (*Stranger On The Third Floor* is an early example), by those lift doors around Mary Astor in *The Maltese Falcon*, or by stair balusters (or even safe deposit boxes in *Fallen Angel*). The final forty minutes of *Suspense* (noir on ice-skates) display a riot of visual effects of this kind: horizontal and vertical stripes from an iron stairway, Venetian blinds as the protagonist contemplates murder in his office and in his apartment, the shadows cast by the curved swords in the heroine's stunt apparatus, the swinging light in a basement confrontation, and the protagonist's reflection in a window turning into the laughing face of the man he has just murdered. With these effects, film-makers made further use of the possibilities of light and darkness to enhance the stories they were telling.

Certain directors are associated with film noir (Fritz Lang, Billy Wilder, Edward Dmytryk, Robert Siodmak, Edgar Ulmer), but, equally, the names of several directors of photography in the opening credits indicate remarkable cinematic skill ahead. The combination of technical developments and deep experience made Nicholas Musuraca, James

Wong Howe, John Seitz, Rudolf Mate, Paul Ivano, John Alton and Robert Krasker masters of their craft, able to give audiences a good awareness of what the very best black and white films look like. Krasker's work on *Odd Man Out* and *The Third Man* is rightly celebrated. John Alton, whose skills enhanced the films he made with Anthony Mann, called his 1949 book "Painting With Light", an indication of how he felt about his art. This book is a remarkably detailed textbook, including suggestions for imbuing mystery through "the phosphorescence of waves in darkness...passing auto lights on ceiling of dark interior... fluctuating neon...a hanging light on the ceiling of gambling joint," and so on. Films noirs photographed by John Alton *(T Men, He Walked By Night, Hollow Triumph, Raw Deal)* are worth seeing for the photography alone.

Authors replicated the dark visual style. Cornell Woolrich's "Night Has A Thousand Eyes" (1945) contains these descriptions: " He craned his neck and looked down the vista of lighted and shadowed strips that were like alternate railroad tiles of black and white....the arc light gave him a drenching flash of surprise as it tore the darkness apart...as they came nearer, it became a silhouette of light farther down the roadway....a coin or two of arc light, no more, fell through the layer of leaves that bowered it and made sequin-like disks on it....For the shadows came from within, and so anything they fell on was shadowed". The combination of director Edward Dmytryk and cinematographer Roy Hunt in *Crossfire* produced a virtuoso array of these effects, with fine use of eye lights (on faces) and diminution of fill lights to create a sharp differentiation between the characters and their backdrop, supplemented by shadows and stripes, creating an immediately arresting opening sequence.

Tilting the camera was another way to reinforce a subjective gaze, a sense that the normal world was off axis. Dutch angles were originally known as Deutsch angles. This showed their German Expressionist heritage, but the name changed when the German nation became a wartime enemy. The discovery of murder in *Stranger On The Third Floor*, the unease in the jazz club in *Phantom Lady,* and, in *Detour*, the flashback to Al's girlfriend after the fatal end to his highway ride, these are all given an additional jolt of disturbance by the use of Dutch angles. *The Third Man* is famed for this feature, deployed so liberally that director William Wyler subsequently presented Carol Reed with a spirit level. Dutch angles make the interrogation in *Strange Impersonation* totally disorientating, culminating in the memorable line "I couldn't have killed Nora Goodrich, I am Nora Goodrich". Angling the camera to bring the ceiling in was another disturbance of equilibrium, as with the emphasis on Moose Molloy's height in *Murder My Sweet*: John Alton used this low-level upward shot extensively in *T Men*. Extreme close-ups of faces heighten the tension in *Desperate* as the clock ticks towards the hour of intended synchronised executions.

In *Laura*, the titular portrait draws detective Mark Macpherson into a growing obsession with someone he has never met (and he is woken from his sleep in front of that picture when she returns from her "death"). Portraits feature often in noir, creating mystery and adding an extra dimension to the narrative. They can be used to lead characters and audiences down false avenues: the portrait in *Strangers In The Night* is of an imaginary daughter, while the picture of Velma in *Murder My Sweet* is also a deception. They can seem to come to life, as in *Laura*: *The Woman In The Window* portrait leads a cerebral college professor into a (literal) nightmare of murder and cover-up. The use of pictures can also become ironic: Edward G Robinson's acclaimed portraits for which he can claim neither credit nor financial reward lead into the bitter denouement of *Scarlet Street*. *Rebecca* and *Phantom Lady* contain portraits of dead women who still loom over proceedings (as do the portraits of Kane which provide a backdrop for the various reminiscences in *Citizen Kane*). In *Sorry, Wrong Number*, the portrayal of the spoiled adult (Barbara Stanwyck, "When I want something, I fight for it and I usually manage to get it") is emphasised by the portrait of her as an indulged small girl above her father's fireplace.

Citizen Kane used an improbable mirror effect in a highly dramatic way. Mirrors echoed portraits in their ability to capture individuals in a different or thought-provoking light, through their emphasis on the duality in people. *The Dark Mirror* made its central theme plain in the title, suggesting the contrasts and interchangeable potential in two sisters once the layers were peeled back (by psychiatrist Lew Ayres in this case). Mirrors showing two faces heighten a threatening relationship between soldiers as they shave in *Crossfire* (as they do with T man and assassin in *T Men*). Multiple mirrors in *Fear In The Night* and *The Lady From Shanghai* emphasise surreal distortion rather than duality.

Music can add an extra dimension to noir, giving the film coherence and providing a guide to expectations and response. Anton Karas' zither in *The Third Man* gives both continuity and striking changes of tone as the Vienna traversed by Holly Martins reveals all its unease beneath fragmented charm. Max Steiner's music for *The Big Sleep* is one of the great film scores, incorporating inquiry and revelation, sexual ease, menace and pursuit, with an optimistic romantic theme which emerges triumphantly at the end. It elevates the studio sets. Miklos Rosza's music for *The Strange Love of*

Martha Ivers skilfully blends romantic themes with menace. Music can signal how noir the narrative will be, as is shown by a comparison between Adolph Deutsch's cues for *The Maltese Falcon* with the more romantic accompaniment for *Moontide*. William Alwyn's leitmotif in *Odd Man Out* heralds the resumption of Johnny's wounded stagger across Belfast, giving it a tragic nobility. The theremin seems a natural musical accompaniment to film noir and it duly turns up in *Raw Deal*, adding to the nervous tension.

Antiheroes and Antiheroines

Humphrey Bogart is often regarded as the archetypal film noir hero, a status founded on *The Maltese Falcon* and *The Big Sleep* (stylistically reinforced in non-noir films like *Casablanca* and *To Have And To Have Not*). His talk is tough and witty. He is self-sufficient, quick and decisive in action, yet with an underlying plan and a survival instinct. He shows considerable grace under pressure, even when tied up or beaten up: a laconic steadfast companion when the bullets are flying. His romantic streak is balanced by realism and a cynical sensibility. He is world-weary, conditioned by his tough experience, but he seeks a principled outcome. He is attractive to and attracted by women, but not significantly distracted by them. He is suitably attired and groomed, not too smart (as the Sternwood sisters remind him in *The Big Sleep*). His vulnerability is there, but well concealed. He is a private eye, surrounded by wrongdoing, but ultimately he is a man of honour (as Raymond Chandler stipulated). He navigates the mean streets and he will continue to do so (probably alone).

This is just one type of noir hero, forged out of the Hammett-Chandler private eye texts (and it is given extra mileage by the appearance of returned veterans on a mission to clear their comrades' names, as with Ladd in *The Blue Dahlia*, Mitchum in *Crossfire* and Bogart again in *Dead Reckoning*). Many male noir protagonists are less purely heroic, lured by obsession or greed, out of control through misfortune or coincidence (especially if Cornell Woolrich has anything to do with it). Robert Mitchum treads the Bogart line in *Crossfire*, giving the pursuit of principle a little extra laconic depth of reflection, while in *Out Of The Past*, filmed in the same year, his performance broadens the range of male leading roles. His character is knocked off course by his obsessive desire for a femme fatale (a not uncommon fate for noir heroes), as his life takes on a doomed trajectory, whereby he can escape neither this obsession nor his past. There is subtlety in his portrayal. It could be that his heroism stays with us longer, since he wrestles with life's challenges in a way that private eyes (whose involvement centres around doing their job) do not. Burt Lancaster, in *The Killers* and in *Criss Cross*, is a good example of a hero doomed by obsession for a woman, the irony given extra edge by Lancaster's impressive physical strength and resilience (echoes perhaps of the Samson and Delilah story).

Noir heroes who come through unscathed, sometimes with the girl, tended to be more complex than their counterparts from pre-war: Borde and Chaumeton, in looking at ambiguity and contradictions in the hero, wrote of being "a long way from the adventure film superman". In *The Maltese Falcon*, Sam Spade is conducting an affair with his partner's wife and his unemotional reaction to Miles Archer's death ("he had no children and a wife that didn't like him") is simply to remove his name from the office sign. In *The Strange Loves of Martha Ivers*, Sam Masterson is chivalrous in his treatment of the vulnerable Toni, but he is also a blackmailer and a double-crossing lover. Paul Madvig, whose success (and ultimate selflessness) in *The Glass Key* we are encouraged to admire, is described as "the biggest crook in the state" in the first minute and later as a "two-fisted newspaperman", given his taste for violence. Nick Blake in *Nobody Lives Forever* ends up with the girl (after he has looked to perpetrate a major confidence trick on her and slapped an earlier girlfriend across the face). Johnny Farrell in *Gilda* is established early on as a chancer and a cheat, his ruthlessness emerging further as the narrative develops. *Johnny O'Clock* is another bad hat hero who is rough with his girlfriend. Significantly, actors with largely unblemished pre-noir styles, such as Robert Montgomery, Fred MacMurray and Tyrone Power, were now able to portray a darker side to their performances. These were heroes with light and dark shading.

Some male protagonists make the wrong (disastrous) choices, usually when swayed by desire: the Swede in *The Killers*, Walter Neff in *Double Indemnity*, Stanton in the carnival noir *Nightmare Alley*. Others are bad through and through, their evil enhanced by the way in which they are filmed, with distorted close-ups from below (*The Maltese Falcon, Crossfire, Touch of Evil*), with their faces out of shot (*Brighton Rock*), and exhibiting an inhuman contempt from on high (*The Third Man*). There are also many cads with whom women fall inexplicably in love (*Strange Illusion, Suspense, They Won't Believe Me, Nora Prentiss*), but these men do not quite seem to have the transformative persuasion shown by femmes fatales.

The changing relationship between men and women can be seen in the noirs where ineffective men are rescued from their difficulties by determined women. The very first noir, *Stranger On The Third Floor*, portrays a resourceful woman coming to the aid of a troubled male protagonist. Ella Raines is proactive in *Phantom Lady* and *The Strange Affair Of Uncle Harry*: there is some suggestion that Joan Harrison, Hitchcock's assistant and then an impressive producer in her own right, might have been a role model for these independent women in noir. Women taxi drivers show positive independence in *Jealousy* and *Two O'Clock Courage*. Women in professional or managerial positions can be agents of positive change: Dr Lorrison in *The High Wall*, Deborah Brown in *The Strange Affair of Uncle Harry*, Ann the lawyer in *Raw Deal* and Dr Ross in *Strangers In The Night*. The empowerment of women was a subtext of classic film noir. Five million women had joined the US workforce between 1940 and 1945 and, although many were laid off when peace came, this shift was recognised in many films noirs.

This empowerment could work both ways. The appearance of the femme fatale is one of the best known features of film noir. Each first appearance was usually memorable (and carefully lit): Barbara Stanwyck in a towel at the top of the stairs (*Double Indemnity*), Jane Greer entering the bar in Acapulco (*Out Of The Past*), Ann Savage by the side of the road (*Detour*), Joan Bennett materialising on the pavement by her portrait (*The Woman In The Window*), Lana Turner entering the truck stop cafe in her white outfit (*The Postman Always Rings Twice*), Lisabeth Scott echoing that entrance in *Pitfall*, Peggy Cummins the sharpshooter in the carnival (*Gun Crazy*), all of these striking scenes probably worth the price of admission on their own. Ann Savage only has around two minutes of screentime in *The Spider*, but she is the most memorable feature of the film. The femme fatale could also dominate the closing scenes in a film, as Gloria Swanson does in *Sunset Boulevard*. As Tony in *Night Editor* puts it to his lover, "You're a female spider…A grade rotten in the flesh, you're bad medicine for me". The original title of *Gun Crazy* was *Deadly Is The Female*, with the poster declaring "Nothing Deadlier Is Known To Man".

These women were more assertive, more intriguing and more dynamic than the men in their films. Marie Windsor said of her femme fatale roles: "I loved playing them because they are the kind of women no one ever forgets". Janey Place wrote that this was "one of the few periods of film in which women are active, not static symbols, are intelligent and powerful, if destructively so, and derive power, not weakness, from their sexuality." Their ruthlessness could be shown in early childhood scenes (*The Strange Woman*, *The Strange Loves of Martha Ivers*) or be revealed as a plot twist later in the film. They achieved entrapment, either through a man's obsessive desire for them or through blackmail (or both). In this way, they enhanced the viewer's perception of their power and their man's enfeeblement. If it was merely a femme fatale's beauty which bound a man to her, she might depart with him. If she entrapped with a view to wrongdoing or revenge, the outcome would be fatal for her. A key location in *Framed* is on a road where the femme fatale plans a murder; the road sign "Dangerous Curve" says it all.

The shifting dynamic between Dan Duryea's blackmailing bully and Lisabeth Scott's femme fatale in *Too Late for Tears* is underlined by his words to her: "Well, Tiger, I didn't know they made them so beautiful and so smart and so hard" and later, "You are a tiger and you've got me in so deep I can't get out." His final expression of this obsessional relationship comes shortly before she poisons him: "Don't ever change, Tiger. I don't think I'd like you so much with a heart".

The potential malevolence of the femme fatale was emphasised by the presence of her counterpart, the good woman, in several films. (*Odd Man Out*, *Brighton Rock* and *The Third Man*, all British noirs, present the loyal and suffering girlfriend without her fatale rival.) The contrasting aspects of womanhood can be emphasised in sisters (*I Wake Up Screaming*, *The Dark Mirror*, *The Big Sleep*) or in stepdaughters (*Murder My Sweet*, *Double Indemnity*). There can be doppelgangers (unrelated look-alikes in *Laura*, *Strange Impersonation*, *Conflict*), which, along with the use of mirrors, provided another way of looking at dual natures. *Raw Deal* emphasises this dichotomy with the "good" woman and the "bad" woman in the same car on the run, and with a voiceover by the "bad" jealous woman. Even when constrained by their "goodness", the moral code displayed by these women, along with their loyalty in all circumstances, is often another facet of empowerment. Peg, the artist in *Body and Soul*, the boxing noir, is a rounded and influential example of the good woman, as is Ann, the lawyer in *Raw Deal*. Lauren Bacall might be the most enigmatic of noir heroines, with a mysterious and hard-won loyalty in several of her roles, but her strength of character is always visible, as in her mission to facilitate escape in *Dark Passage*.

Films noirs were notable for the full drawing of their secondary characters. Peter Lorre, Sidney Greenstreet and Elisha Cook Jr set an early high standard in *The Maltese Falcon*. Often these characters are memorable villains, either physically striking like Greenstreet, Laird Cregar, Raymond Burr or Mike Mazurski, or simply powerful personalities, such as George Macready or Thomas Mitchell. There are also older controlling women, such as Judith Anderson, Helene Thimig or Dame May Whitty. We encounter distinctive sideshow personalities in dark streets or shady rooms on the way: Harry Lime's duplicitous associates, the whimsical Belfast characters in *Odd Man Out*, those who might know Larry Cravat in *Somewhere In The Night*, the good-time girl and her "husband" in *Crossfire*, all of Raymond Chandler's characters, Lee Cobb as a sceptical lawman or newspaperman, the gallery of grotesques in The *Lady from Shanghai*. The cinematic language of noir establishes the lasting impression made by many of these individual actors in light and shade.

Contemporary Concerns

"Funny things happen inside people's heads" declares Sidney Greenstreet as the psychologist Dr Mark Hamilton in *Conflict*. Later in the film, he describes psychoanalysis as "the proper application of pure science". Film noir brought the life of the mind to the forefront of public imagination, building on the increased interest in psychology (the study of the mind) and psychiatry (the branch of medicine which aims to diagnose and treat mental conditions) over the previous thirty years. Noirs were fairly relaxed about the distinction between the two disciplines. Lee Cobb in *The Dark Past* seems to move effortlessly from being an upstate college professor of psychology to becoming a top police psychiatrist in New York City. The femme fatale in *Nightmare Alley*, who uses her professional status to bring about the antihero's downfall, is a consulting psychologist. Protagonists are released from institutions (*Rage In Heaven, Ministry of Fear*), sometimes temporarily (*Phantom Lady*) or unfairly incarcerated in them (*Shock, The Locket*). A psychiatrist or psychologist could be the hero, solving a tangled mystery (*Conflict, The Dark Mirror*) or talking a psychotic killer around in a lakeside cabin (*The Dark Past*). *Hollow Triumph* plays with mistaken identity, doppelgängers and impersonations, "the Freudian subconscious", sibling envy, and textbooks on clinical and abnormal psychology; the violent robber central character has "practising psychoanalysis without a licence" listed among his previous offences.

Famously, in 1924 Samuel Goldwyn offered Sigmund Freud $100,000 to come to Hollywood "to write a love story for the screen". This uneasy meeting of serious psychological study and commercial cinema (Freud refused) only began to bear fruit twenty years later, as Hollywood started to explore the life of the mind in screenplays. Borde and Chaumeton assert that "after 1939 many Hollywood producers' names were to be found on the list of subscribers to The Psychoanalytical Review". European immigrants fuelled interest in the profession. Producers and actors consulted psychoanalysts such as May Romm and Karl Menninger. Mental turmoil in films could be a simple device to bring horror, as it had been in *The Cabinet of Dr Caligari*, or, increasingly in the 1940s, as an explanation for murder or other criminal activities. Nino Frank in 1946 used the phrase "criminal psychology". This could be seen as a way of helping to understand the real-life atrocities of the mid-twentieth century, individual and collective, of which the cinema audience would have been aware. Menninger was one of several psychoanalysts who protested at the simplification of their profession in films and the critic Bosley Crowther wrote that *Shock* did a disservice to psychiatry when so many of those affected by World War Two had need of it. *Whirlpool* centres its narrative around the battle of wits between a distinguished psychoanalyst (and loyal husband) and a manipulative fraudulent hypnotist (a "cheap parasite").

Amnesia was a frequent condition in noirs. Lee Server describes amnesia as "noir's version of the common cold". This could be seen as evidence of cinematic interest in the life of the mind (or simply as a plot device). It can last a long time ("You left me in the winter, it's now Spring" in *Street of*

Chance). It can be a trick to confuse someone (*My Name Is Julia Ross*). The film's narrative may be a protagonist's quest to find out who he really is (*Two O'Clock Courage, Somewhere In The Night*) or whether he committed a murder (*The High Wall, Black Angel*). It might be connected to post-war PTSD (*The Chase, The Blue Dahlia*). It is a common occurrence which does not ring entirely true with modern audiences, particularly when it seemed that an injection with sodium amytol ("narcosynthesis") could produce instant recall in the criminal or the innocent amnesiac (*The High Wall, Possessed*).

The officers of the law encountered by Phillip Marlowe are rough round the edges, occasionally corrupt: "Stick your nose into my business and you'll wake up in an alley with the cats looking down on you". Corruption was a seam running through many noirs. The prison in *Brute Force* is run by a weak Governor and an evil sadistic Chief Warder. Elected law enforcers were fallible: in *The Strange Loves of Martha Ivers*, the compromised husband says that "in a small city like this, as DA, you get to feel like God". The corruptibility of the police is shown by the recruitment of one as a killer in *Johnny O'Clock*: "Take a cop who earns a couple of hundred a month and use him". Sometimes, as in *Phantom Lady*, the police behave in a sufficiently threatening and dishevelled manner to be indistinguishable from a gang of crooks. Noir detectives were prone to the same disastrous obsessions as anyone else (*I Wake Up Screaming, Fallen Angel*). The absence of law enforcers in so many noirs helped to create the atmosphere of nihilism and moral uncertainty, particularly evident in the mid-1940s window between American filmmakers' stance against ideological enemies, first Nazism and then Communism.

During this intermission between the perception of external threats, concerns over society's imperfections at home tended to produce one of two reactions in film-makers, either cynicism, as shown by Chandler and Wilder, or a subtext of political awareness, as shown by Adrian Scott, the producer, and Edward Dmytryk, notably through their messages in *Crossfire*. This left-leaning sensibility was rooted in the culture of the New Deal and an anti-fascism which extended to a wartime alliance with Communist Russia. Abraham Polonsky, later blacklisted, was a committed Marxist. Although this is not obvious, either in the boxing noir he wrote (*Body and Soul*) or the racketeering noir he directed (*Force of Evil*), the tendency of money to corrupt people and structures in these films might now be seen as an indictment of capitalism. After 1947, there was a perceptible swing to the right, with the nine days of House of Un-American Activities Committee hearings into the Hollywood film industry, the "Hollywood Ten" (who included Dmytryk and Scott), and the blacklist of 300 artists. If film noir after 1949 has any political messages, they are more conservative in tone.

Law-breaking policemen could bring difficulties with the Code, which required that figures of authority should be treated with respect, with corruption a very exceptional occurrence. Working round the Code, as Dmytryk implied, was a challenge for film-makers, but one which brought out ingenuity and nuance, contributing to the enduring quality of many noirs from this period. The censors were confronted with a wartime and immediately post-war landscape which was more cynical and more sexually aware, as readily portrayed on film. It felt an unsettling time for many Americans. Unsurprisingly, the post-war divorce rate reached a high in 1946 at 4.3 per thousand people, rising from 3.5 the year before and falling to 3.4 in 1947 (it had been under 2 in the

1930s and was around 2 in the 1950s). Premarital pregnancies doubled in the US between the early 1940s and the late 1950s.

The film-makers were expected to work within the parameters of the Motion Picture Production Code, first agreed in March 1930. The Code was divided into two parts: General Principles and Particular Applications. The General Principles stated that no picture should lower the moral standards of those who see it and that there should be no ridiculing of the rule of law (and no sympathy created for its violation). The Particular Applications set out the specific restrictions. First were Crimes Against The Law. Brutal killings could not be presented in detail. The technique and methods of crime (murder, safe-cracking, dynamiting trains, arson included in this list) could not be presented in a way which might inspire imitation. "The use of liquor in American life, (when not required by the plot or for proper characterisation) will not be shown". The second section dealt with Sex. "Adultery, sometimes necessary plot material, must not be explicitly treated or justified or presented attractively." Excessive and lustful kissing, lustful embraces, and suggestive postures and gestures were not to be shown. Rape could never be more than suggested, while sex perversion and miscegenation were forbidden. The remaining ten sections dealt more succinctly and generally with Vulgarity, Obscenity, Profanity, Costume (no nudity, undressing, undue exposure while dancing), Dances, Religion, Locations, National Feelings, Titles and Repellent Subjects. This last included "a woman selling her virtue".

The intense eroticism of many films noirs is created by a combination of sublime lighting and camerawork on the one hand and, on the other, working round this ban on explicit references to sex. Pierre Duvillars described this as "the supreme refinement of an eroticism that dares not speak its name" (L'Eroticisme du Cinema, 1951). Suggestion could be achieved through replacing action with loaded dialogue, as has been shown (discussion of racehorses in *The Big Sleep* and speed limits in *Double Indemnity*). Articles of clothing could be indicators of seductive availability (the anklet in *Double* I*ndemnity*, gloves (which are then removed) in *Gilda*). There could be a discreet edit to imply what had taken place between the two scenes, with mounting attraction (sometimes accompanied by as lingering a kiss as allowed) in the first, and post-coital serenity in the second (Dorothy Malone's bookshop in *The Big Sleep*). Sharing a cigarette allowed imagination of the intimacy to follow. This was where greater interest in psychology and the representation of forbidden desires blended in noir, with dreamlike sexuality and symbolism. Erotic scenes in film noir have generally worn well.

Looking at the Code's concerns about specific films gives an idea of the particular interests of the censors and the manoeuvring required of film-makers. In *The Maltese Falcon*, the Office required the removal of any sense of a sexual relationship between Sam Spade and his client Brigid O'Shaughnessy. It also insisted that the homosexuality of Joel Cairo (Peter Lorre) be concealed (along with less drinking generally and cutting out some of Sidney Greenstreet's expostulations). In *Laura*, there was a similar concern over any hint of a sexual relationship between Laura and Waldo Lydecker. The casting of Clifton Webb (gay of manner as an actor and off-screen) as Waldo must have helped with this: his reception from the bath of Dana Andrews in the opening scene might also have alerted the Board to another interpretation. The Production Code Authority report on *Murder My Sweet* reminded the producers that "there must, of course, be nothing of the 'pansy' characterisation about Marriott" and that escaping punishment by committing suicide was not acceptable. Joseph Breen had first been confronted by "Double Indemnity" in novel form in 1935: he wrote to interested studios to object to the murderers cheating the law by dying at their own hands, the improper treatment of an illicit and adulterous relationship, and the showing of the details of a vicious and cold-blooded murder. Another Breen letter, in 1947, to producer Dore Schary gave tentative approval to *Crossfire* with the following stipulations. First, racial epithets would be removed from the film's dialogue. Secondly, references to drinking and drunkenness would be toned down "wherever possible". Thirdly, there would be no suggestion that Ginny, the befriending girl, is a prostitute nor that the older man in her apartment is a customer. Fourth, there would be "nothing of a 'pansy' characterisation about Samuels or his relationship with the soldiers". Fifth, RKO would agree to "make certain that nothing in the finished picture will cause any complaint from the War Department".

Nuance and suggestion made the meanings still more powerful and lasting as film-makers steered a way through objections like these. There is enough hint of homosexuality in Cairo's manner and Bogart's reaction to his scent, in Marriott's brief cameo, and in Samuels' solicitude towards the younger soldier (while the homophobic aspect of *Crossfire* was changed to anti-Semitism). (The Yiddish-origin word "gunsel", used three times in *The Maltese Falcon*, has a homosexual meaning, but neither Hammett's editor nor the censors were aware of this and so it stayed in.) Ginny's profession in *Crossfire* is hardly masked to the modern viewer. In *Scarlet Street*, Fritz Lang dressed Joan Bennett in a plastic raincoat and placed her under a lamppost (receiving a beating from a man who was clearly her pimp). The Code may have been appalled by prostitution, but its existence was undeniable. The ending of *Scarlet Street* caused problems for the Administration, given the proposed suicide and the perception of justice thwarted. A failed suicide attempt, destitution and eternal mental torment (confirmed by a policeman passer-by) proved an acceptable solution which replicated the original Renoir French version of 1931. Film-makers were able to make a virtue of what could not be shown: the femme fatale's facial expression as brutal murder was committed out of shot again made it an enduring memory (*Double Indemnity, Framed*). These subtle ways of showing continue to enhance the films which utilised them.

The 1950s

John Huston's brilliant robbery noir, *The Asphalt Jungle*, released in 1950, gives an indication of the changing backdrop ahead. The action, seen entirely from the gang's perspective, has neither uncertainty nor fateful choices: the criminals (given human qualities by Huston) are simply doing their jobs. Their women are needy and powerless, rather than fatale. James Ellroy's definition of film noir ("A man meets a woman and it goes wrong") does not apply here. There are further signs of how the 1950s might unfold: reinforcement of law and order (the police commander's concluding speech on the value of a police force and the rarity of bad apples within it), new icons (the film includes Marilyn Monroe in a very early role) and emerging youth culture (teenagers dance beside a jukebox near the end). Some standards are maintained: the three gang members carrying out the elaborate subterranean heist keep their hats on throughout.

John Huston, *The Asphalt Jungle*'s director, met Sterling Hayden, his leading actor in the film, in Washington when they were both protesting against the House of UnAmerican Activities investigation into "subversives" in the film industry. Anxiety about a Red threat at all levels of society had a significant influence on American cinema in the 1950s. Blacklisting took out a number of creative contributors to the early post-war films and it flagged warning signs in front of studios and producers. J Edgar Hoover, Director of the

FBI, objected to the "lack of patriotism" in the leading character in *Pick-Up on South Street*, even when opposing communists. He demanded a meeting with Daryl Zanuck from Twentieth Century Fox and Sam Fuller, the director. When his requested changes were not made, all references to the FBI were removed from the film and the studio's relationship with the Bureau was broken.

Government agents, notably the FBI, were invariably honest and courageous. Policemen were not always so: weariness, envy, impulsiveness and disillusionment could send them to the bad, as in *Where The Sidewalk Ends*, *Kansas City Confidential*, and *The Prowler*. The corrupt and murderous policeman, depicted by Joseph Losey and Dalton Trumbo in the last of these, is the work of two people blacklisted shortly afterwards.

The ambiguities in so much earlier film noir now became more black-and-white. What one might call "public service noir" appeared after the war in *The House on 92nd Street* and *The Street With No Name*, but these films proliferated in the 1950s as "Cold War offerings" were encouraged and American institutions celebrated (such as the US Postal Service and its agents in *Appointment With Danger*). *Southside 1-100* opens with a stentorian five minute voiceover about the Korean War: "The world is split into two camps. The fight will be to the death. The time for words is over; we are fighting back with weapons...There is one weapon behind all these weapons:, this is the most powerful of all: the American dollar....the strength and the health of a nation depend on the value of its currency...so the integrity, the honesty of the dollar must be protected...and this function falls to a branch of the Treasury Department, the United States Secret Service". The replacement of a personal subjective narration with the authoritative tones of a newsreader was part of this move towards what were in effect public service promotional films.

Film noir was less prominent through the 1950s as other entertainment strands developed. Television, in particular, was a disruptive force: cinema audiences halved between 1946 and 1956. Promising film noir themes were taken up in series form on television, a development which has continued ever since. Television, combined with the 1948 Supreme Court ruling which ended block booking, led to a diminution in the number of B pictures. Technical developments encouraged the idea of cinema spectacle (partly as a response to the threat of television): a four-fold increase in the number of films made in colour through the single-strip process, CinemaScope and Cinerama with their increase in screen size, and experiments with 3D cinema. The advent of drive-in cinema brought a younger clientele, at whom an increasing number of films were directed: the director Nicholas Ray and the actor James Dean were at the forefront of this.

Robert Aldrich's *Kiss Me Deadly* in 1955 included the private eye (Micky Spillane's Mike Hammer), Los Angeles as a location, a complex plot (drug dealers in the novel become nuclear thieves in the film to circumvent censorship issues) and stylised direction with a bleak ending. It was banned in the UK, loved by French critics and revered in hindsight by other writers on film. It is remarkable, but it sits outside the mainstream of 1940s noir, looking forward to the French new wave and, even more, to the 1960s in its sports cars and consumerism, its cultural references in art and music, the sadism and deliberate immorality of its hero (with his exploitation of failing marriages), the sexual availability of its women, and its atomic age anxieties. The bright lighting throughout the film prefigures its explosive and apocalyptic finale. *Murder By Contract*, a stylish B film from 1958, directed in seven days by Irving Lerner, a previously blacklisted editor, ploughs the same terrain, depicting outdoor Los Angeles by daylight. Again, it looks forward, probably to arthouse noir, rather than back: Martin Scorsese cited it as the film that had influenced him most.

Mike Hammer, as portrayed by actor Ralph Meeker, is more of a protagonist than a hero: assertive, notably with women, brutal, unprincipled and physically imposing. Sterling Hayden's characters, central to two of the finest 1950s noirs, *The Asphalt Jungle* and *The Killing*, are in the same mould. His focus is entirely on planning the elaborate heist and *The Killing*'s structure, brilliantly layered by Stanley Kubrick, ensures that the audience is also solely interested in that. These are antiheroes of a different kind, portrayed in a black and white landscape, which underscore the Manichean nature of those films, either as a committed criminal with a brutal streak (*The Asphalt Jungle*, *The Killing*) or as an immoveable law enforcer (*Crime Wave*, *Crime of Passion*). His bravura performance as Jack D Ripper in *Dr Strangelove* could perhaps be seen as a parody of 1950s concerns when he plays a US Air Force General who launches a nuclear strike in the belief that Communist Russians have made him impotent by putting fluoride in the water supply.

There were still intensely dark films in the 1950s (*The Big Combo* inhabits all the shaded territory of old), but daytime location shooting began to change the look of many crime films, a trend anticipated by *Woman On The Run* (San Francisco), *The Naked City* (New York) and *Sunset Boulevard* (Los Angeles) at the end of the 1940s. An increasing use of outdoor daylight filming inevitably diluted the noir element of films. The streets of New York provided a distinctive backdrop in a significant number of films including *Side Street* and *Killer's Kiss*, while endings in the Mojave Desert (*The

Prowler) and the snows of Wyoming (*Nightfall*) further opened out the palate of crime films. Realistic location shooting moved further from the stylised look and language of noir (and further from the legacy of German Expressionism).

The Production Code was less rigorously enforced as the !950s unfolded. Joseph Breen retired in 1954. Challenges came from several directions: Otto Preminger, supported by United Artists, over explicit references to virginity in *The Moon Is Blue*, Samuel Goldwyn demanding a revision of the Code in 1953 ("The world has moved on, but the code has stood still.") and the appearance of foreign films which were not subject to the Code. An illustrative detail of changing times can be seen in the increasing depiction of married couples in the same bed (as opposed to separate beds). Film noir had needed to use subtlety to circumnavigate the Code, but there was less need for subtlety and erotic suggestion now.

The films noirs of the 1950s were more explicit in their depiction of sex because they found they could be. The imprecise fear of Communism led to a sharper delineation of good and bad in many films, along with a veneration of government agencies and agents. Technological developments provided a greater range of visual expression, leaving behind the dark confined interiors of many 1940s films. There are some fine films noirs throughout the 1950s, with work from established directors and photographers (Robert Siodmak, Joe Lewis, Fritz Lang, John Alton, Carol Reed, James Wong Howe) alongside new influences (Robert Aldrich, Sam Fuller, Stanley Kubrick). However, the balance was different, with the language of noir just one of many styles in American film-making and new concerns at the forefront of stories.

The decade does end with a film noir from the very top drawer. If Orson Welles paved the way for film noir with *Citizen Kane*, he provided its coda with *Touch of Evil* (1958). Heavily stylised and intensely dark, the film shows numerous noir traits: Expressionist influences, subjective camerawork, enigmatic characterisation, memorable minor characters in a complex plot, the otherness of borderlands and Latin America, an emphasis on interiors and confined spaces, Marlene Dietrich as an observing femme fatale, and a superb score by Henry Mancini. *Touch of Evil* was recognised internationally at the time and has grown in reputation since then. Eddie Muller writes how Welles had "set the cinematic syntax for film noir: the quest for truth in morally ambiguous terrain, the cynical take on the corrupting influence of power, the off-kilter visual style...Watching *Touch of Evil* is like drinking vintage wine before it turns to vinegar".

Classic?

Do the years 1946 to 1948 mark "the ascension and apogee" of film noir, as Borde and Chaumeton assert (with the 1949-1950 chapter entitled Decadence and Transformation)? Some of the most iconic noirs were made before or after this period, so it seems prescriptive to create a short window of classic film noir. [Borde and Chaumeton are natural organisers into groups or eras, as is shown by their placement of noirs in specific categories: Criminal psychology, Social tendencies, Gangsters and so on.] As has already been suggested, the three years immediately after the war were years without any sense of political mission against external and threatening forces, so one can perhaps see a less filtered mirror on American society in films of this time. However, if the cinematic language and the subject tone are what define film noir (as Roger Ebert put it "It's not what a movie is about, it's how it is about it"), then the whole 1940s decade should be included, with continuing noir delights through until Touch of Evil.

The critic Stephen Armstrong has suggested a parallel with the (Italian) Renaissance in the way artists, working together in an industrialised (studio) system, possessed "talent (that) was so intense that around the edges, they were creating something remarkable...a body of work of real quality." There was, of course, a noir reference to the Renaissance beneath the Prater Wheel in *The Third Man*, where Orson Welles' Harry Lime suggested that creativity emerged from conflict rather than "peace and brotherly love". Welles would have been delighted by this comparison.

There are, perhaps, even greater similarities with another era of artistic flowering, the Golden Age of Dutch painting in the seventeenth century. This was an era of technical mastery, volume of production (with an estimated 1.3 million paintings produced between 1640 and 1660), provision for a mass market, with contemporary, unostentatious and secular subject matter (if of a rather more serene nature in the Dutch world). The artists were more interested in output than in artistic theory. The artists' guilds (named after St Luke, the patron saint of artists) controlled who could sell and trade paintings, echoing the studio control of film noir. The manipulation of light and shade was a notable feature: Van Gogh described Franz Hals' 27 different shades of black (a close parallel with noir's mastery of black and white). Women were depicted more frequently and often on a more equal basis in these pictures. There were suggestive hints in many of the paintings, apparent to contemporary and subsequent audiences: Vermeer's women with their letters or billets doux, the depiction of domestic maidservants and their possible availability, and the presence of musical instruments which signified an amorous encounter.

Significantly, the remarkable artistic merit of the Dutch Golden Age was only realised in looking back after it was over. It might be stretching a point to compare James Wong Howe or Nicholas Musuraca to Jacob van Ruisdael or Jan van Goyen, Robert Siodmak or Edward Dmytryk to Pieter de Hooch or Aelbert Cuyp (even if John Alton's "Painting With Light" paid tribute to Rembrandt's skill with dark backgrounds and selective lighting). Nonetheless, it might be possible to see the Golden Age of film noir as presenting a mirror to the world of the 1940s with compelling artistry in the same way that Dutch artists did for the 1640s. Both these distinctive collective representations were only properly recognised artistically years and even decades after their time.

The events portrayed in films noirs were (well) outside the life experience of those who watched them in the 1940s, but the undercurrents were of their time and relevant to life in the USA: the impact of world war, the destabilising of family life, the increasing agency of women, the effect of urbanisation and economic uncertainty on community, the awareness of sexuality, the interest in psychological explanations, and a more cynical attitude to authority figures. Many of these themes seemed to recede during the Eisenhower years of the 1950s, with conservatism, consumerism, conformity, suburbia and the restatement of family life all apparently more to the fore (even though the steadily rising crime rate suggests that the outward appearance masked other trends in society). Wilder, Dmytryk and the rest would not have seen themselves portraying features of contemporary society (nor would the Golden Age Dutch artists), but film noir captured those 1940s tensions within absorbing narratives, depicted in a distinctive and artistic style.

The poet and novelist Nicholas Christopher starts his book on film noir by recounting the overwhelming effect on him of seeing *Out Of The Past* in a Paris cinema at the age of 22. He describes the film as managing to "deposit me for a charged, magical stretch of time in the maze of downtown San Francisco on an ink-dark night, surrounded by menacing, jagged shadows, crystalline shafts of light, and men and women who were partly phantoms and partly larger-than-life (like people in a dream) shortly after the Second World War". Seeing any of the "best" fifty films noirs in a sufficiently good print and on a sufficiently large screen is still a reminder of what they reveal to us and how brilliantly they reveal it.

Stranger On The Third Floor
the dream sequence in the first acknowledged film noir

The Maltese Falcon (1941)
"You certainly are a most headstrong individual". Sydney Greenstreet heads an array of memorable secondary characters

Phantom Lady (1944)
clear Expressionist influence from Robert Siodmak

Phantom Lady (1944)
another example of Expressionist composition

Double Indemnity (1944)
"There's a speed limit in this state, Mr Neff."

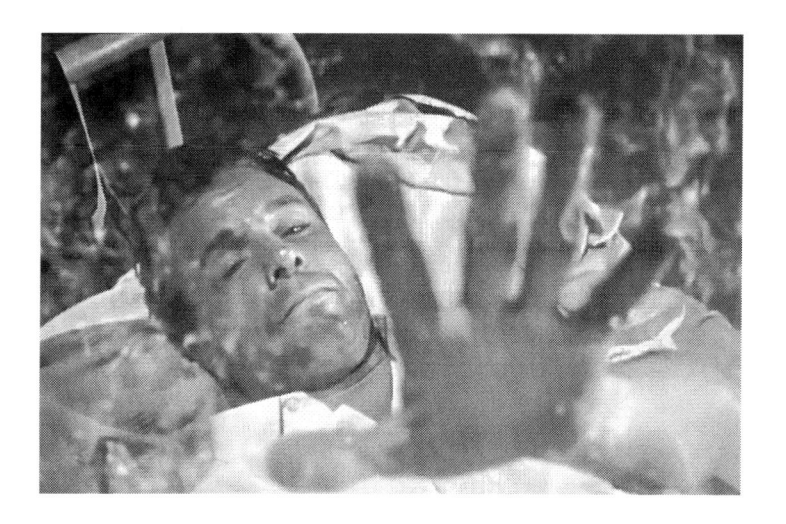

Murder My Sweet (1944)
"A Black Pool opened up at my feet and I dived in"

The Woman In The Window (1944)
Portraits were features of a number of films noirs

Detour (1945)
Edgar Ulmer's Depression-tinged B picture

Scarlet Street (1945)
Joan Bennett's attire and location make
her profession evident as she surveys her fallen pimp

The Third Man (1949)
rubble noir

The Blue Dahlia (1946)
Buzz struggles with PTSD

Somewhere In The Night (1946)
Post-war amnesia: George Taylor
tries to find out his real identity

The Big Sleep (1946)
Vivienne "I don't like your manners"
Marlowe "I don't like them much myself"

The Killers (1946)
"A man meets a woman and it goes wrong"

Framed (1947)
an appropriate road sign beside
which to plan a fatal car accident with a lady

Suspense (1946)
noir on ice

The Postman Always Rings Twice (1946)
a memorable first appearance

Crossfire (1947)
Gloria Grahame's streetwalker
and the anxieties of the Breen office

Lady In The Lake (1947)
The camera as Philip Marlowe: the only times
we see Robert Montgomery are in mirrors

The Dark Mirror (1946)
several noir themes: Lew Ayres'
psychiatrist as the problem-solving hero,
a striking contrast between "good" and "bad" girls,
and Olivia de Havilland as twin sisters

Out Of The Past (1947)
Nicholas Musuraca's lyrical photography

The Third Man (1949)
the photography of Robert Krasker,
while Dutch angles reflect the upheaval
in Holly Martins' understanding

Sunset Boulevard (1950)
subjective narration from beyond the grave

Act of Violence (1948)
the bar scene which replicates
Edward Hopper's "Nighthawks"

D.O.A (1950)
"I don't think you understand, Bigelow. You've been murdered."

The Big Combo (1955)
John Alton's ability to "paint with light"

Touch Of Evil (1958)
The celebrated opening sequence
and the "otherness" of Latin America

Twelve Films Which Take Film Noir into and Through the 1950s

The Asphalt Jungle
Night and the City
Side Street
The Prowler
Kansas City Confidential
The Big Heat
The Big Combo
Kiss Me Deadly
The Killing
Nightfall
Murder by Contract
Touch of Evil

Bibliography

John Alton: Painting With Light
Peter Biskind: Easy Riders, Raging Bulls
Raymond Borde and Etienne Chaumeton: A Panorama of American Film Noir
James M Cain: Mildred Pierce
James M Cain: The Postman Always Rings Twice
Charlotte Chandler: Nobody's Perfect, Billy Wilder, A Personal Biography
Raymond Chandler: The Lady in the Lake
Raymond Chandler: The Long Goodbye
Nicholas Christopher: Somewhere In The Night
Charles Drazin: The Faber Book of French Cinema
Paul Duncan: Film Noir
Ed Paul Duncan and Jurgen Muller: Film Noir
Quentin Falk: Travels in Greeneland
Dashiell Hammett: The Glass Key
Susan Hayward: Cinema Studies: The Key Concepts (fourth edition)
Allan V Horwitz and Gerald N Grob: The Checkered History of American Psychiatric Epidemiology (Milbank Quarterly, December 2011)
Steven Jacobs: The Dark Galleries: A Museum Guide to Painted Portraits in Film Noir, Gothic Melodramas and Ghost Stories of the 1940s and 1950s

Sarah Kozloff: Invisible Storytellers: Voice-Over Narration in American Fiction Film
William Luhr: Film Noir
Russell Merritt: Crying in Color: How Hollywood Coped When Technicolor Died (Journal of the National Film and Sound Archive, Australia, Volume 3, No 2/3, 2008)
Eddie Muller: Dark City, The Lost World of Film Noir
James Naremore: More Than Night
Janey Place: 'Women in Film Noir', in Women in Film Noir, (ed) E Ann Kaplan,
Dilys Powell: The Golden Screen, Fifty Years of Films
Gerald Pratley: The Cinema of Otto Preminger
Graham Petrie: Hollywood Destinies, European Directors in America, 1922-1931
Dominic Sandbrook: Mad As Hell. The Crisis of the 1970s and the Rise of the Populist Right
Andrew Scull: Madness in Civilization: A Cultural History of Insanity
Andrew Spicer: Film Noir
David Thomson: A Biographical Dictionary of Film
David Thomson: Have You Seen?
Ginette Vincendeau: Deep Focus: How the French birthed film noir (Sight and Sound 2016)
Robin Wood: Howard Hawks
Cornell Woolrich: The Night Has A Thousand Eyes
Cornell Woolrich: Waltz Into Darkness

Acknowledgements

Many thanks to my team of editors, James Barr, Dugald Young, James Grant Peterkin and Akadil Belgara, for all their help with this piece of writing. Errors, omissions and design failings that remain are all down to me.

Still photographs from various films noirs are included for the purpose of comment and criticism. Only one or two stills from each film are included, with the intention of encouraging readers to watch the whole work. In the same spirit, references to specific observations made by other film writers should be seen as an encouragement to read their work cited in the bibliography.

Printed in Great Britain
by Amazon

accb9c04-7641-45e4-bce5-275ded22a649R01